# Large Logo Diesels in View

**Gavin Morrison**

Rails

# Introduction

In 1965 the British Railways Board decided on a new corporate image and adopted Rail blue as the standard colour for its locomotive fleet together with a new double arrow symbol. In 1978 it was agreed that a further change was desirable and selected classes were repainted with a large logo and full wrap round yellow nose ends or cab fronts, the first machine to be treated being Class 56 No 56036. This simple alteration transformed the look of the locomotives and, in spite of all the new colour schemes that have appeared in recent years, for the author at least the large logo livery is one of the best. He illustrates it here with a selection of his many photographs. In the compilation of the book, Lawrie Bowles has given very valuable help with the captions.

Gavin Morrison

*Front Cover:* Having recently been on Royal train duties, class 37/4 No 37421 is in immaculate condition as it passes the gorse bushes just to the south of Helmsdale station on the 6.35 from Inverness to Wick and Thurso on 1st July 1987. The locomotive details are on page 9.

*Title Page:* On 21st March 1987, 47407 crosses the River Calder between Ravensthorpe and Dewsbury on the 13.00 Bangor-York with a Regional Railways liveried Mark 2 with Trans-Pennine branding. 47407 was one of the first batch of the class built, as D1506, to Finsbury Park in January 1963, being renumbered in March 1974. It was named *Aycliffe* on 8th November 1984, losing the plates in May 1988. A Gateshead loco from 1979, it transferred to Immingham on denaming. It was allocated to HQ and stored in August 1990 and withdrawn in March 1994, being broken up at Frodingham depot in December 1995 by MRJ Phillips.

*Right:* This section of track used to have four lines and was part of the three miles of the 'Speed' signalling system introduced by the LMS in 1932. It was never introduced anywhere else but survived until 1973. The three miles extended from Heaton Lodge junction in the west to Thornhill junction in the east. Now with only three tracks it is very busy and occasionally causes delays. To the left of the picture is the site of the old steam shed which closed in 1967, then coded 56D. The shed and yard site have now become a housing development. The picture is impossible to take today without a pole or drone due to the trees and undergrowth. Class 56 No 56120 is heading a Cawoods box container coal train probably for Liverpool, the coal being destined for Ireland. No 56120 entered service on 29th May 1983 and was withdrawn in December 2003.

Published by Rails Publishing
www.railspublishing.com

Printed in the EU

# Contents

| | |
|---|---|
| **Scotland** | **4** |
| **North Eastern Region** | **24** |
| **Eastern Region** | **40** |
| **Southern Region** | **52** |
| **Western Region** | **59** |
| **London Midland Region** | **76** |

# Scotland

37420 *The Scottish Hosteller* arrives at Georgemas Jct with the 06.35 from Inverness to Wick and Thurso on 30th June 1987. Partly hidden by the footbridge is the Cl.37 which will take the Thurso portion onwards. Since 2012, the site of the platform to the left of the picture has been used as a railhead freight facility. New as D6997 to Cardiff Canton in 1965, it was renumbered 37297 in March 1974 and rebuilt to a Class 37/4 in December 1985 before transfer to Inverness. This train was a regular duty until transferred to Thornaby in 1990. It then received InterCity Mainline livery and subsequently Provincial colours in March 1997 before storage in 2000 and sale for scrap in January 2008.

*Above:* 37420 has now detached from its train from Inverness at Wick and run round to take the 12.00 back to Inverness. The Highland Omnibuses, now part of Stagecoach, is to the left of the picture. 30th June 1987.

*Below:* 37418 has taken its train to Thurso and detached prior to running round. New as D6971 in 1963 it was renumbered 37271 in March 1974 and transferred from South Wales to Scotland in February 1984. Rebuilt to Cl.37/4 37418 at Crewe in November 1985, it was named *An Comunn Gaidhealach* in October 1986. It spent most of its time on the Kyle of Lochalsh line but did make appearances on the Far North services. It left Scotland in 1990 and lost its name in February 1991, becoming *Pectinidae* next month. It then worked Cambrian, North Wales and Lancashire services. It lost *Pectinidae* for a month in 1992, becoming *Gordon Grigg*. It finally lost *Pectinidae* in March 1993 before becoming *East Lancashire Railway* in 1994, by then in EWS maroon. It saw service in Scotland again from 1999 but was stored in September 2007 and sold for preservation in February 2008, moving to the East Lancs Railway in March 2009. It was restored to National Rail records in July 2017 as available for main line work as a preserved locomotive. 30th June 1987.

Between Invershin and Culrain stations, the Far North Line crosses the Oykel, or Shin, Viaduct over the River Oykel. Here 37260 crosses the viaduct on 3rd July 1987 with the Inverness-Lairg tanks. 37260 was built as D6960 in January 1965 and served in the Eastern Region, gaining full yellow ends on its green livery. Renumbered 37260 in December 1973 it was transferred to Scotland in 1982, allocated to Inverness and fitted with RETB equipment that May. It was named *Radio Highland* on 7th July 1984, but lost that in August 1989 after suffering fire damage which caused its withdrawal that month. It was broken up at MC Metals, Shettleston, Glasgow in August 1991.

37262 *Dounreay* on the Royal Scotsman train, with LNWR-liveried coaches, this being a BR Mk1 BSK, and 37415 on the 11.10 Kyle of Lochalsh-Inverness meet at Dingwall station on 19th April 1986. The junction between the Kyle and Far North Lines can be seen above the rear Mk1 coach. 37415 was another of the class, as D6977, allocated to South Wales when new. It became 37415 in November 1985 when fitted with ETH, RETB etc. It lost Large Logo livery in May 1990 after an overhaul, going into InterCity mainline colours. At the time Inverness had only four steam-heated Class 37s, with this one working well. The Mark 1 coaches on the service train were electrically heated by then. 37262, so numbered in February 1974, gained large logo livery and RETB on transfer to Scotland in 1982. Stored on occasions from 1999, it was withdrawn and stripped at Wigan CRDC and officially withdrawn in 2001, being broken up at Sims Metals in 2004.

*Above:* 37262 again, at Inverness this time on the Rose Street triangle of lines, with the Sunday Newspaper van train to Lairg. This was, until 2005, the only train on the Far North lines on a Sunday. In the background are Inverness Station, on the right, Lochgorm Works and the diesel depot is on the left. The third side of the triangle, bypassing the station, is in the foreground. 5th July 1987.

*Below:* 37418 reappears, this time on the Kyle of Lochalsh line. It has just passed through the Stromeferry avalanche shelter on the 16.40 Kyle to Inverness. The leading vehicle of the train is Metro Cammell Class 101 DMU driving trailer 54356, converted in 1987 to run loco-hauled as an observation car on the Kyle line. It was painted in a green and cream livery and numbered 6300 in 1988. After withdrawal it was privately preserved and is presently at the Barry Tourist Railway, under its original number 56356. 24th September 1988.

*Above:* 37421 was built as D6967 in 1965 allocated to Darnall, Sheffield. It became 37267 in May 1974 and was rebuilt to Cl.37/4 in December 1985 when it went to Scotland. It was requested for Royal duties (see cover) but it continued in ordinary service in very clean condition. It is seen here at Garve on the 17.55 Inverness-Kyle on 29th June 1987. It was named *Strombidae* in 1991 and spent time on Cambrian and Lancashire services. Renamed *The Kingsman* on 9th November 1993 it was then in BR Petroleum Sector livery. Withdrawn in March 2009 after it had been sold for preservation to L&S Locomotives and then used on the Pontypool & Blaenavon Railway. It was sold on to Colas who returned it to main line traffic in December 2014 in Colas yellow livery. 29th June 1987.

*Below:* D6991 was one of the South Wales batch delivered in 1965, which became 37291 in March 1974 and 37419 when rebuilt to Cl.37/4 specification in December 1985 when it moved to Scotland in Large Logo livery. It is seen here on 2nd September 1988 by Loch Achanalt, between Achanalt and Achnasheen on the 11.10 Inverness to Kyle, now with Mk2 passenger stock. It was repainted to InterCity Mainline livery in September 1990 when it returned south. EWS livery followed in 2009 and DRS livery in 2011. After a spell on the Cumbrian Coast, since mid-2015 it has worked mostly in East Anglia on the Norwich to Lowestoft and Great Yarmouth services. 2nd September 1988.

*Above:* 37414 was built as D6987 in 1965 as part of the South Wales batch. It became 37287 and then 37414 on rebuilding as a Cl.37/4 in October 1985 for use on the Inverness north routes. It is seen here on maintenance inside Inverness depot, the former Highland Railway Lochgorm Works on 19th April 1986. It left Scotland in May 1989 and was named *Cathays C&W Works 1846–1993* on 1st January 1994. By then it had gained Regional Railways livery. It went to store in March 2000 and was sold to BRE Ltd for preservation in 2005 and moved by road to the Weardale Railway. It was not to be and was removed by road for scrap to Thomson, Stockton on 10th March 2009 and broken up. 19th April 1986.

*Below:* A gathering of locomotives outside Inverness Diesel depot on 19th April 1986, showing Class 26 No 26026 in Railfreight grey livery and class 37/0s Nos 37262 *Dounreay* and 37260 *Radio Highland* plus Class 47/4 No 47614. This picture was taken from the now demolished Welch's Bridge signal box.

37260 *Radio Highland* is seen here leaving the passing loop at Slochd Summit on the Highland main line with an Inverness-Millerhill freight on 6th July 1989, shortly before the fire damage that caused its withdrawal the next month. The railway is parallel with the A9 road, much less busy then than today. Even then a caravan was causing a traffic queue!

A little further south on the main line, the A9 crosses the line on a modern bridge. 37418 *An Comunn Gaidhealach* leads the 09.33 Glasgow Queen St to Inverness on 7th July 1989 under the bridge.

On 10th June 1988, 47517 heads the 08.35 "Clansman" from Euston to Inverness via Birmingham, which by this time is formed of air conditioned Mk.2 coaches, three of which have already been painted in the incoming InterCity 'raspberry ripple' livery. It is north of Dalwhinnie station, with the Dalwhinnie distillery in the background, owned since 1987 by United Distillers. Rail distribution had ceased in 1969. 47517 was built in November 1965 as D1975 and was renumbered 47517 in April 1974. It was named *Andrew Carnegie* in August 1985 and became RES 47758 in March 1994 when it lost Large Logo livery. Renamed *Regency Rail Cruises* in September 1998 and lost it in May 2001. It was withdrawn in March 2004 and scrapped at Booth Roe, Rotherham in April 2008.

Some 8 miles south of Dalwhinnie, 37118 passes Druimuachdar Summit, at 1480ft the highest pass on the national system, on 29th August 1988 with the mid-day Inverness-Mossend freight. Built as D6818 in March 1963, it was new to Darnall (Sheffield) and was renumbered in February 1974, gaining this livery in 1987. Shortly after this photo was taken it was renumbered 37359 and allocated to the Petroleum and Chemicals pool at Eastfield. It was stored unserviceable in 1994 and never worked again. It was purchased for spares by Harry Needle in August 2002 and broken up at Carnforth in January 2005, although it was not officially withdrawn until August 2006.

*Above:* This was one of the mammoth weekend tours run by 'Pathfinder' around this period and named 'Caledonian'. It departed Reading on Friday arriving at Wick around midday on Saturday. It then travelled to Dufftown and Invereness and on to Edinburgh. On Sunday it visited Polmadie depot in Glasgow and then to Carlisle. A trip south on the Settle-Carlisle followed to Leeds and then back to Carnforth. It was then onwards to Birmingham and eventually Reading. At this stage of the tour class 37/0s Nos 37025 and 37245 were in charge and are shown climbing to Druimachdar summit (1480 feet). 11th June 1988.

*Below:* Class 47/0 No 47280 in Railfreight Grey livery has just passed the remote level crossing and signal box at Carmont just over 5 miles south of Stonehaven. It is hauling the 12.15 Aberdeen Guild Street to Mossend on 7th March 1990. It entered service in December 1965 numbered D1982 and carried the unofficial name *Pedigree* between January 1986 until withdrawn in February 1999. It was sold to Fragonset and stored at Kineton MOD depot.

47644 *The Permanent Way Institution* approaches Arbroath station on 24th June 1989 on the 08.55 Aberdeen-Plymouth 'Devon Scot', the rake of InterCity-liveried Mk2 air conditioned coaches marred only by the blue & grey Mk1 BG at the front. New as D1923 in December 1965, it was one of the few Brush Type 4s allocated to the Southern Region to displace steam when almost new. It became 47246 in February 1974 and gained Large Logo livery when converted to Cl.47/4 in February 1986 numbered 47644. The name was added four months later and removed in December 1990. After withdrawal in July 1991 and reinstatement seven months later it was reallocated to Rail Express Systems and gained its livery in January 1994 as 47756. It was named *Royal Mail Tyneside* in July 1995. Withdrawn again in March 2004 it was broken up by Ron Hull Ltd, Rotherham in May 2006. Arbroath is also home to Scotland's oldest miniature railway, Kerr's, just to the south of the station running alongside the main line.

The 12.25 Inverness to Glasgow Queen Street on 22nd May 1987 is seen leaving Dunblane behind 47656. The DMU alongside forms the local service to Edinburgh or Glasgow. 47656 was built as D1719 in February 1964 and became 47128 in April 1974. Modified as a Cl 47/4 in June 1986 it became 47656, but three years later it was further modified as a Cl.47/8 in InterCity Swallow livery as 47811. It then went into First Great Western Green on transfer to Landore. It was stored in January 2008. It was used as a super shunter by Freightliner at Crewe Basford Hall yard but then became disused again.

A dramatic view of 37405, then named *Strathclyde Region*, was another of the South Wales batch, new as D6982 in May 1965, renumbered 37282 in March 1974 and transferring to Scotland in 1984, before being rebuilt to Cl.37/4 specification as 37405 in September 1985 and named in April 1986. It left Scotland in 1993 and later worked in North Wales and Lancashire. It lost Large Logo livery in favour of InterCity Mainline and then EWS maroon. It was back on West Highland services from the end of 1997 till 2003 with spells on the Settle & Carlisle and Cardiff Valleys services following. Now in the hands of DRS, and in its livery, it regularly works East Anglia services from Norwich. Here the 16.50 Glasgow Queen St-Fort William passes the Sighthill flats shortly before turning west at Cowlairs. Built between 1964 and 1969, demolition took place at Fountainwell in 2008/09 and Pinkston between 2013 and 2016.

*Above:* On 14th July 1989, 20227 in railfreight grey with large logo, 20054 in standard blue and 37410 in Large Logo blue livery, rest at Eastfield depot. 20227 is currently preserved by the Class 20 Locomotive Society, and operating on the mainline painted in a very attractive crimson lake London Underground style livery. It was the last built Class 20, in February 1968 as D8327, renumbered 20227 in December 1973.

*Below:* On 15th June 1985, 37111 heads the 14.15 Fort William-Glasgow Queen Street past Cowlairs starting the descent to the terminus. Cowlairs is now the site of the signalling control centre for most of west Scotland's rail network, which opened in December 2008. 37111 was built as D6811 in February 1963. It was named *Loch Eil Outward Bound* from 1985 to 1986 and then *Glengarnock* from 1988 to withdrawal. Transferred to Scotland in January 1978 it spent most of the rest of its working life there. Renumbered 37326 in 1986 for working Railfreight Metals from Motherwell, it reverted to 37111 in 1989. Passed to TransRail strategic reserve it was stored in April 1996 before withdrawal in September 1998. An attempted preservation scheme came to nothing and the loco was scrapped at EMR Kingsbury in July 2003.

*Above:* 37111 *Loch Eil Outward Bound* is shown again, earlier the same day, hauling the previous night's 22.10 Euston-Fort William at Ardlui. Behind the loco is 'ETHEL' 97250. When the electrically-heated Mk3 sleepers took over from steam or dual heated Mk1s, the Cl.37/0s on the West Highland line could not supply the necessary current. So before the advent of the ETH Cl.37/4s, the temporary solution was to convert three redundant Cl.25 locomotives in acceptable condition into mobile generators to work with the Cl.37s. This is 97250 *ETHEL 1*, the former 25310, converted in June 1983. With blue-painted cabs, they were not able to pull trains. They lasted until mid-1986 when enough Cl.37/4s were available, but then found a few years further use providing power for such as steam specials with electrically heated coaches. They were stored at Inverness, but then all three were taken to MC Metals, Shettleston, Glasgow and broken up in August 1994.

The same train is now seen at Bridge of Orchy a little under an hour later. The third vehicle is a Mk1 BSO converted to miniature buffet car by removing a bay of seats and placing a refreshment trolley there.

*Above:* A view of what was then Fort William depot on a snowy 29th March 1987 with 20102, 37412 and 20206 and two other Cl.37s awaiting their next duties. To the left is the line onwards towards Mallaig crossing the River Lochy. 37412 *Loch Lomond* originated as D6601 of the South Wales fleet and became 37301 in March 1974, being rebuilt to Class 37/4 37412 in October 1985. It gained its name in March 1987, shortly before this photo was taken. It lost it after transfer to Laira in 1989 and became *Driver John Elliot* in January 1995. Its work was then in Wales and the South West until stored in October 2002. Sold to Harry Needle in 2008 it was stripped and went to EMR Kingsbury for scrap in 2012.

*Below:* 37411 *The Institution of Railway Signal Engineers* is seen here on the 16.05 Fort William-Mallaig on 10th June 1988 along the south side of Loch Eilt between Glenfinnan and Lochailort. New in June 1965 and renumbered from D6990 to 37290 in March 1974 and converted to Cl.37/4 37412 in Large Logo blue livery in October 1985, it gained its name in May 1987. It spent most of 1989 away from Scotland, and left again late in 1990 after transfer to Laira when it lost its name. In Wales it gained the name *Ty Hafan* in May 1997 (removed March 2001) but returned to Scotland in 1999, and was renamed *The Scottish Railway Preservation Society* in April 2001. It left again in 2003 for a spell in Yorkshire and on the Settle & Carlisle, and then headed back to South Wales, being renamed *Caerphilly Castle/Castell Caerffili* in November 2005. A much reliveried locomotive, after green and rail blue, Large Logo followed in 1985, but by 1998 it was in EWS livery, which lasted until repainted back to green as D6990 again in August 2005. It was stored in June 2006 and gained TransRail grey colours that September. Out of service in 2010, it went to Booth, Rotherham in February 2013 and was cut up that May.

*Above:* Here we see 26035 outside the former steam shed at Ayr on 7th June 1988. BRCW Type 2 D5335 was renumbered 26035 in December 1973 and received Railfreight grey livery with large logo. It was withdrawn at the end of 1992 having received the 'Dutch' livery of grey with a yellow band in 1991. It is flanked by Metro Cammell DMUs 101304 in Strathclyde orange and black livery and 101353 in blue and grey, together with Class 08 shunter 08561. New to 64B Haymarket, Edinburgh in July 1959, it was loaned to 34B Hornsey for Kings Cross suburban services from new until June 1960 when it went to Inverness. At its last overhaul, in 1985, it received air brakes but lost its train heating boiler so became basically a freight locomotive. After withdrawal, the Class 26 went to McWilliams, Shettleston but was rescued for the South Yorkshire Railway, but is now to be found on the Caledonian Railway at Brechin, back in rail blue, awaiting restoration to traffic. The line from Glasgow Central to Ayr was electrified in September 1986 using new Class 318 units, supplanted from 2014 by Class 380 on most trains.

*Below:* The next day, 8th June 1988, similar 26038 approaches Dumfries station with a down PW train, passing the site of the former steam shed on the left. New in August 1959 to Haymarket it avoided the loan to London and stayed there until February 1960 when it also went to Inverness, staying there for 26 years. It received Railfreight grey with large logo at its last overhaul in May 1986, with similar mods to 26035. It too received 'Dutch' livery before withdrawal in October 1992. It went for store at the South Yorkshire Railway and is now preserved, based at the SRPS Diesel Group and is on long-term loan to the North Yorkshire Moors Railway.

*Above:* Here seen outside Haymarket depot on 25th July 1981 are 47711 *Greyfriars Bobby* and 47712 *Lady Diana Spencer*; they were very early examples of the Class 47s to receive large logo livery. Both were named on 30th April 1981. 47711 was new as D1941 in June 1966 and became 47498 and then converted to Cl.47/7 specification for Edinburgh-Glasgow push-pull working in September 1979. The name was removed in December 1990 on transfer to Network SouthEast at Old Oak Common, but before it left it gained ScotRail livery. It was renamed County of Hertfordshire in September 1993. Further livery changes saw it in Network SouthEast colours by 1990 and finally Virgin Trains. Withdrawn in 2000 it was cut up by Harry Needle at Toton in September 2004. 47712 fared better. New in August 1966 as D1948 it became 47505 in February 1974 and then 47712 in November 1979. It was transferred to Crewe in November 1990. Its name was removed in April 1995 but it subsequently carried *Dick Whittington*, *Artemis* and *Pride of Carlisle*. Passing to the Tyseley Museum in 1997, it regained its *Lady Diana Spencer* name at the Crewe Gresty Lane Open Day on 23rd July 2016 and is back in ScotRail livery. Based at the Weardale Railway it is main line certified.

*Below:* The 133-year old, 244-yard Penmanshiel tunnel, near Grantshouse, Berwickshire, was undergoing improvement works on 17th March 1979, when it collapsed, sadly killing two workmen. As the ground was too unstable to repair the tunnel, a short deviation to the East Coast Main Line was built to the west of the original. 1100 yards of the old main line were abandoned and the tunnel sealed. The new works were opened on 20th August that year. Seen here on the new line is 37508, with the large logo on Railfreight grey with a northbound aluminium train on 16th September 1987. Built as D6790 in January 1963, it became 37090 in December 1973, and 37508 in May 1986 on modification to Cl.37/5. It then became one of the locos selected for working with Eurostar trains and it became 37606 in July 1995. It remains in service, now with DRS on nuclear fuel traffic based at Carlisle Kingmoor.

# North Eastern Region

*Above:* BREL Crewe-built 56124 was new in September 1983 in Large Logo livery. It is seen here approaching the Blyth Road Bridge, the A189, at Cambois, North Blyth with an empty coal train on 20th March 1992, having lost its Blue Circle Cement nameplates. It subsequently carried Trainload Coal and Transrail liveries before being overhauled by Brush for Fastline Freight with reliability improvements which led to it being renumbered 56302. As such it is still working on the main line, on hire to Colas, briefly named *Wilson Walshe* and then *Peco The Railway Modeller*, and in Colas colours.

*Below:* With their nose ends coupled, Railfreight grey with large logo and red solebars, 20132 and 20010 enter Scarborough on the 'Vladivostok Avoider' railtour on 12th May 1990; the tour ran from Sheffield via Penistone to Scarborough. The train used 8 Mk1s with two Mk.2b BSOs in the middle and the return, with 20010 leading, visited many freight lines on the way back. 20010 was new as D8010 in October 1957 as part of the first batch allocated to Devons Road Bow. It gained this livery in 1985 but was withdrawn in December 1991 and broken up at MC Metals, Shettleston in January 1994. D8132 was built in March 1966 and renumbered 20132 in 1973. It is still active on the main line in 2017, including transferring London Underground trains between Bombardier Derby and West Ruislip.

Redmire Quarry is pictured here on 30th April 1990, with 37514 and 37517 on a stone train ready to depart. Rail traffic to the quarry ceased in December 1992 and after a last special on 2nd January 1993, the line remained closed though the MoD was interested in using the line for access to Catterick Camp. They paid for restoration of the line and the construction of an access point at Redmire. The Wensleydale Railway Association was formed in 1990 with the aim of running a passenger service again, for the first time since 1954. A trial train was run in 1993 and MoD operations started in 1996 and continue. Under the Wensleydale Railway plc, public services restarted in 4th July 2003 reaching Redmire in 2004, running to a new station at Northallerton West. 37514, new in February 1963 as D6815, became 37115 in May 1974 and was modified to Cl.37/5 as 37514 in March 1987, gaining this livery then. In April 1995 it was selected as one of the Class 37s to work with Eurostar, receiving all the necessary coupling mods, a repaint into Eurostar grey and renumbering as 37609. In July 1997 it was reallocated to DRS for Sellafield work. Repainted in DRS blue, it remains allocated to Kingmoor working occasional passenger trains. 37517 was new in June 1961 as D6718, one of the first batch of this class working initially from Stratford. It became 37018 in February 1974 and was modified as above to 37517 in April 1987. In and out of store in the early years of the 21st century, it was bought by West Coast Railway Co in 2007 and officially withdrawn in January 2008 and remains in store at Carnforth in Loadhaul livery.

56086 is seen here working a Merry-go-round train at Whitley Bridge Junction, en route to Eggborough power station on 16th February 1990. It was new in December 1980 and was later named *The Magistrates' Association* in October 1995, but was withdrawn in September 2008 and passed to the Shackerstone Railway where it received blue livery with large logos. It was reinstated at the end of 2011, but then sold to Europhoenix in August 2012. Finally withdrawn in February 2013 it was cut up next month at EMR, Kingsbury.

*Above:* 56076 in the red stripe version of Railfreight large logo livery is seen here leaving Monk Fryston yard with a Merry-go-round train on 25th July 1990. Built at Doncaster works in April 1980, it carried the name *Blyth Power* from September 1982 until October 1986. It was still nameless when this picture was taken but gained *British Steel Trostre* in May 1993, retaining this until withdrawn in September 2008. It was broken up at Booth, Rotherham in February 2009.

*Below:* Still at Monk Fryston yard, but on 29th August 1991, we see the 16.22 Hull Dairycoates-Swinden Quarry, near Grassington North Yorkshire, headed by 31180+31247, both in the livery shown above. 31180 was built as D5601 in March 1960, gaining its new number in December 1973. Withdrawn in September 1996, it languished out of use until reinstated in February 2000, probably for a move to a scrapoyard as it was withdrawn again a week later. It was broken up at T J Thomson, Stockton in June 2003. 31247 was new in December 1960, becoming 31247 in December 1973. It lasted in use until withdrawn in February 2000, but met its fate at the same time and place as 31180. Thomson itself stopped taking ferrous scrap in December 2016 and held an auction in February 2017 which included number panels from many locomotives broken up there!

*Above:* On 3rd May 1987 47426 hauls the diverted 14.10 Newcastle-Poole past the old Signal Box at Cudworth, Chapeltown Line Junction. The passenger service to Cudworth had ceased in 1968 but diverted trains continued to use this route until closure of the old Midland Main line route south of here in the following month due to mining subsidence. 47426 started life as Brush Type 4 D1534 in August 1963 becoming 47426 in February 1974. It was named *Dibatag* in July 1990, retaining this until withdrawal on 15th December 1992 still in this livery. It was cut up at Old Oak Common in May 1997.

*Below:* Class 37s 37116 in large logo livery and 37244 in Railfreight Distribution sector colours at Normanton, Goose Hill on 6th August 1992 on the well-loaded 18.30 Stourton (Leeds)-Southampton freightliner. New as D6816 in March 1963 it gained the new number in February 1974. Named *Comet* on 20 November 1989, it lost this in favour of *Sister Dora* on 25th February 1996, which it retained until withdrawn in February 2007. By May 1987 it had received full yellow ends and an intermediate-sized logo, replaced by the full large logo livery at classified overhaul in June 1988. In 1992 it was transferred to Tinsley as an extended range loco. Stored serviceable briefly in 1993 it then moved to Inverness for passenger work and then to Motherwell for coal traffic later in 1993. Transrail acquired it in May 1995, based at Bescot. Stored in December 2001, by then in Transrail colours, it was sold for preservation to the Chinnor & Princes Risborough Railway in 2007, and subsequently acquired by Colas in January 2014 and overhauled at Barrow Hill for its operational fleet, being reinstated to traffic at the end of 2014 in full Colas orange and yellow livery. D6944 was new in September 1964 for South Wales coal traffic. Renumbered 37244 in February 1974 it went into the Railfreight Distribution pool at Tinsley in May 1991. Briefly with Network SouthEast it then joined EWS but was stored unserviceable in February 1999 and cut up at Wigan.

Due to engineering works between Leeds and Wakefield Westgate on 18th April 1992 the 15.50 Leeds-Kings Cross was diverted via Hunslet where 91025 and its rake of Mk4 coaches tailed by DVT 82209, was being hauled by 47481 in large logo livery. D1627 was new in October 1964 and became 47481 on 20th May 1974. It was named *Sunstar* from 18th November 1990 until withdrawal in April 2003. It was cut up at Sims Metals, Beeston that July.

47458 is seen here on the Regional Railways 12.52 Liverpool-Newcastle on 5th August 1989, soon after leaving Leeds, in the Marsh Lane cutting a little to the west of Neville Hill. The loco was new as D1578 in May 1964 and became 47458 in February 1974. At this time it was allocated to Bristol, but after overhaul in 1990 it was transferred to Rail Express Systems and was painted in its red and grey colours, receiving the name *County of Cambridgeshire* at Bristol Bath Road on 2nd December. The nameplates were removed in May 1993, it was withdrawn to HQ the next month and formally withdrawn in May 1994, being scrapped at Booth Roe, Rotherham in February 1996.

Still in Leeds, we have an overview of the yard at Holbeck depot, which was on the site of the former steam depot. In the background is the viaduct which used to carry the LNWR route to Manchester, and in latter years the ECML to Doncaster. The viaduct has been out of use for years. In the depot on 17th September 1990 were 47488, new as D1713 in January 1964 and became 47488 in February 1974, being named *Rail Riders* on 9th August 1988, losing this name in August 1992 and gaining *Davies the Ocean* on 18th January 1995. It was withdrawn in October 1993 and reinstated in December 1994 and again withdrawn between February and March 1995 after which it was reported as owned by Waterman Railways and in its livery. It then passed to Fragonset Railways and repainted in its BR dual green colours. It was moved to Barrow Hill in December 2003, then to Carnforth in April 2007 and back that October. It went to Burton on Trent in December 2013. 47482 is seen above attached to one of the short-lived Class 141 DMUs. New as D1636 in December 1964 and renumbered in June 1974. Shortly after this photo, it was transferred to RES and moved to Crewe. Out of traffic in October 1993 and withdrawn in May 1994, it was broken up by MRJ Phillips at Crewe Works in June 1995. To the left is an unidentified Class 47/4 and nearer the camera is Class 101 DMU 51463 behind 37408 *Loch Rannoch* which was new as D6989 in June 1965, becoming 37289 in February 1974. It was another selected for conversion to Cl.37/4 and was outshopped from Crewe in August 1985 when it was moved to Eastfield for West Highland work. It gained its name on 1st September 1986. After a Crewe overhaul it was transferred to Cardiff in May 1989 and on to the Departmental Civil Engineer at Immingham in November 1989. Two weeks after this photo, it returned to Cardiff for more passenger work before moving to Eastfield in January 1991 but worked to Kyle and Inverness-Aberdeen. In July 1992 it moved to Grangemouth for Petroleum traffic and rapidly on to Immingham, but remained on ScotRail passenger traffic and then to Crewe for passenger traffic. In June 1997 it was transferred to Transrail and then to Immingham, returning to passenger work from Crewe in November 1998. It went to EWS Motherwell in April 2000 and fitted with RETB. Back to Cardiff in November 2001 it was on Cardiff Valleys work until August 2003 when it moved to Crewe for Yorkshire passenger work. It then went back to Cardiff Valleys in December 2004 but suffered extensive damage in a collision with parked coaches on 1st August 2005 at Rhymney. It went into the EWS Tactical reserve fleet but stored for stripping next month. Officially withdrawn in January 2008 it was scrapped by EMR, Kingsbury that month.

On 10th July 1990, 47434 approaches Morley, south of Leeds, and its 5569-yd long tunnel with an evening Newcastle-Liverpool express, formed on Mark 2 stock in blue and grey or Regional Rail colours. The open ground behind the train was used in steam days for storing carriages needed only for summer services. New in October 1963, D1549 was renumbered 47434 in June 1974 and received large logo livery in 1985. It was named *Pride in Huddersfield*, losing this in January 1991 when it was taken out of traffic and withdrawn the following month. It was broken up at Booth Roe, Rotherham in November 1993.

*Above:* Seen at Horbury, just east of Healey Mills yard, 37519 hauls the Glazebrook-Haverton Hill tanks on 21st January 1989. It is in large logo Railfreight livery with the red band. New as D6727 in September 1961 and renumbered 37027 in December 1973 and remained in East Anglia until transferred to Eastfield in April 1980. At St Rollox, Glasgow Works, the loco was seen on 27th August 1981 in an experimental blue with full yellow ends livery but with small numerals. The wrap-round yellow was soon removed but It was named *Loch Eil* in October. Its boiler was isolated in April 1986 and it lost its name on 1st February 1987. After overhaul at Crewe works, it was modified to Class 37/5 and renumbered 37519 in July 1987, emerging in the livery seen here, with the addition of the Thornaby Kingfisher logo. It was allocated to Freight Metals at Thornaby when photographed, soon moving on to Railfreight Steel at Motherwell and then Trainload Metals at Immingham in 1992. Several other moves in the north east followed before a move to EWS Toton in September 1997. Passenger work resumed by July 1999, but was short-lived, being stored that November. It was allocated for use in France on contract hire at the end of 2003 and withdrawn in August 2007. Moved from Eastleigh to Booth, Rotherham on 18th February 2008 it was cut up there on 7th March.

*Below:* The Tinsley Kingfisher logo also appears on 47363, which has the full height large logo and a white stripe at cantrail level. It was pictured in Horbury cutting working the 10.26 Weaste-Port Clarence tank train on 9th March 1990. The deep cutting beyond the loco was an opened-out tunnel. It was new in July 1965 as D1882, and being a freight loco with no heating, was renumbered 47363 in February 1974. It was named *Billingham Enterprise* on 6th December 1985, this being removed in October 1991. In July 1991 it was allocated to Railfreight Distribution at Tinsley in Railfreight two-tone grey. It became 47385 on 12th July 1994 when fitted for multiple working but reverted to 47363 on 16th October 1995. Stored in 1999 and withdrawn in July 2000, it was reinstated to Fragonset at Derby but was in stored status by August 2007. It was cut up by Booth, Rotherham in March 2010.

*Above:* 47434 is seen again, this time at Huddersfield station, appropriately for its name (see p.32), on 23rd April 1990. It is seen from above the tunnel at the west end of the station on the 14.20 Newcastle-Liverpool. In the background is the famous George Hotel where the Rugby League was formed in 1895.

*Below:* 47473 is seen in Paddock Cutting, west of Huddersfield on the 08.50 Liverpool-Newcastle on 15th May 1988. This area was formerly quadruple tracked. New as D1601 in July 1964 to South Wales, it was renumbered in January 1974 and was allocated to Gateshead when photographed. Late in 1990 it was allocated to the Parcels sector and went on to InterCity West Coast Infrastructure in 1992, to Trainload Freight in March 1994 and then stored in 1995. Reinstated at Crewe in August 1996 and withdrawn in October 1997, it was broken up at Crewe Works by MRJ Phillips in March 1998.

56098 and 56021 are seen whilst on track relaying duties at Marsden on 6th November 1983, some half a mile east of the entrance to Standedge Tunnel. In large logo colours, 56098 contrasts with the standard blue on 56021. 56098 was built at Doncaster Works in October 1981. Allocated to Tactical Reserve at Immingham in December 2003. It was withdrawn in August 2005 and sold to the Northampton & Lamport Railway. It was reinstated to the Network Rail computer at the end of December 2011 to UK Rail Leasing and is in Railfreight grey carrying the name *Lost Boys 68-88*, applied on 15th January 2016.

On 27th June 1986 the Sandoz Drug Co, an American pharmaceutical company with a base at Camberley, Surrey, organised an outing for its guests to York. It used the VSOE Pullman rake, hauled by 47460, and is seen here passing the site of Laisterdyke station, closed in 1966. It was on a stretch of track between junctions leading to Bradford Interchange, Leeds (still open) and closed routes to Queensbury, Keighley and Halifax (the Queensbury routes), a direct line to Bowling and Halifax, and links to lines to Shipley and Dudley Hill, all now closed. 47460 was built in May 1964 as D1580 and renumbered in February 1974. It had been unofficially named *Great Eastern* by Stratford Depot staff on 3rd April 1978, despite BR's ban on named locos which had lasted since 1967. The name was removed on 20th, but the ban soon ended. On 6th March 1991, again unofficially, it received the name *Triton* at Tinsley, losing the name on 7th February 1992. It passed to the Parcels sector at Crewe at the end of 1991 but was withdrawn in January 1992, reinstated and withdrawn again the next month. It passed to Booth Roe, Rotherham in April 1993 and scrapped there in May 1994.

On 8th October 1989, Newcastle-Liverpool trains were being diverted via the Calder Valley route. 47536 is seen here just west of the site of Brighouse station, closed 5th January 1970 but reopened on 28th May 2000, hauling Regional Railways' 12.13 Newcastle-Liverpool. Built as D1655 in January 1965, it was allocated 47071, but never carried it as it was rebuilt to Class 47/4 as 47536 in October 1974. The following month it was allocated to Railfreight Parcels at Crewe. From 2nd December 1990 it carried the unofficial name *Solario*. In April 1997 it was allocated to TransRail Reserve fleet and withdrawn for disposal in April 2004. It was cut up at Booth Roe, Rotherham on 7thth October 2005.

Class 56 No 56078 *Doncaster Enterprise* is passing the east end of the site of the once busy marshalling yard at Brighouse in West Yorkshire on 24th March 2004 heading the 6E33 10.57 Knowsley-Immingham tanks. At this time it was one of the last of the class 56s in service. It was new in May 1980, withdrawn in September 2010, sold to Colas and reinstated at the end of 2012. The name was applied on 27th September 2003 and removed at the end of 2004.

Here we see the prototype of Class 47, then Brush Type 4 on 17th April 1988 leaving Halifax on the diverted 10.50 Liverpool-Newcastle Transpennine service, seen from the lower part of Beacon Hill, not far above the tunnel entrance. The large building on the skyline is the former HQ of the Halifax Building Society and by the coal drops to the right, which still exist, is the former junction for the GNR line to Keighley and Bradford whilst the goods yard at the back of the station is now an upmarket children's play building named Eureka. D1500 was taken into stock on 28th September 1962 at Finsbury Park and was one of the first locos to feature electric carriage heating, the batch being nicknamed 'Generators'. It became the forerunner of the 512-strong class. Displaced from East Coast main line duties by the introduction of air-braked stock, it was fitted in 1971 and returned to front line duties. In October 1973 it became 47401. Displaced by HSTs, it was allocated to Gateshead, and on 16th December 1981 it was named *North Eastern* as seen here. However, that was removed a few days later when transferred to Immingham. The run-down of the class started in 1986, and included the generators as non standard. However, as 47401 had just received an overhaul into large logo livery, it survived and was allocated to Provincial sector for Trans-Pennine work, then Departmental, and in February 1990, Trainload Freight for Humberside oil trains. It also received a hybrid standard blue/large logo livery with the number D1500 reinstated. It was named *Star of the East* in May 1991. A minor overhaul followed with repaint into original BR green. Eventually withdrawn on 5th June 1992, early in 1993 it was acquired by the 47401 Project and gained large logo livery again in 1994 and its *North Eastern* name the following year. It is still based at the Midland Railway Centre.

*Above:* A long-lost feature of railway working was the parcels and newspaper train, and one of the best-known was the Red Bank Van train which on weekdays ran from Heaton to Manchester Red Bank, just outside Victoria station, with empty vans from the previous night's newspaper deliveries. 22-23 vans were normally run which in steam days required double-heading, but here we see 47456 with approximately half that load just outside Bradford Interchange on 10th April 1988 on a diverted working. D1576 entered service on 25 April 1964 and became 47456 in March 1974. A long-term resident of Carlisle Kingmoor, it had transferred to Crewe Diesel in 1987, where it remained until stored in September 1991 and withdrawn that October. It was cut up at Booth, Rotherham in May 1993.

*Below:* In the days before electrification of the Aire Valley route, through trains from London to Bradford Forster Square had to be diesel-hauled from Leeds, but with the Class 91 remaining attached. Here 31174 hauls 91006 and its train as the 19.33 Bradford-Kings Cross on 3rd August 1989. Brush Type 2, later Class 31, D5594 was new in March 1960, renumbered 31174 in September 1998 and cut up by Harry Needle at EMR, Kingsbury in June-July 2001.

# Eastern Region

Absolutely fresh ex-works at Doncaster, 50036 is ready to leave the sidings just south of the station with a test train to Peterborough and back on 23rd May 1986. This view taken from a bridge over a dual carriageway shows the Works in the background with the former excursion platform to the left. Electrification catenary has now made the view much less open. Originally leased by BR, D436 was new on 12th August 1968, it was for West Coast Main Line services north of Crewe, from where they were displaced by electrification. BR acquired the locos in 1977/1978. The whole class moved to the West Country to displace diesel hydraulics. The class became very popular with enthusiasts and was nicknamed "Hoovers". Their life on the Western Region was relatively short because of the introduction of HSTs and they were reallocated to other duties. Reliability problems led to the class being refurbished between 1979 and 1983. After the first six, they were all outshopped in large logo livery as shown here. Many received Network SouthEast livery later. On displacement, they were used on other services from Paddington, and on the Waterloo-Exeter route, where they were eventually concentrated. With continuing reliability problems, replacement by Cl.47/4s began and withdrawals started in 1987. D436 became 50036 in 1973 and was named *Victorious* on 16th May 1978. An early refurbishing, it gained its second coat of this livery just before photographed but was withdrawn on 12th April 1991 still in this livery, and scrapped at Booth Roe, Rotherham in July 1992.

This view looking south from the north end of Doncaster station was taken from the road bridge which once carried the Great North Road (A1) through the town before the by-pass was built. The train is the 8.55 Penzance-Newcastle headed by class 47/4 No 47503. Full details about the locomotive appear on page 95. 1st May 1986.

Class 58 was a modular construction locomotive on which work started in 1979 at Doncaster. The use was for Merry-go-round trains and the first, 58001 is seen here in the works having gone back in for attention after trials on 26th April 1983, having been launched on 9th December 1982. The first ten of the class finally entered service in February 1984. The loco was the first to carry this livery, basically the same as large logo blue but using grey instead, with different cab colouring. Use of the class, which all passed to EWS on privatisation, dwindled with the decline of coal traffic, and all were out of traffic by 2002. It was in Mainline grey from 1994 until withdrawn, but was back in large logo grey by 2006. 32 of the class were then sent to Europe for further use in the Netherlands, France and Spain. 58001 was withdrawn on 8th October 1999 and after 10 years of storage, it was exported to France in August 2009 but it is stored there at Alizay in ETF France colours of yellow with white roof, green bodyside stripe, blue sole bar & ETF branding.

*Above right:* Still in Doncaster Works, this is 50041 *Bulwark* in the aftermath of its accident on 23 November 1983 when it approached Paddington on a sleeping car train from Penzance at 60mph and derailed under Bishops Bridge Road and turned on its side at the end of the platforms. It was recovered and sent to Doncaster for repairs. It was new on 3rd October 1968 as D441, was renumbered in 1973 and gained large logo livery at refurbishment. After the accident it spent 1984 being rebuilt, underwent a test train on 4th January 1985 and re-entered traffic on the 23rd. It then lasted until withdrawn on 17th April 1990, being broken up by Coopers Metals at Old Oak Common July next year.

*Below right:* A group of locos outside Doncaster Works on 26th March 1986 showing 56098 and 56112, with freshly painted 50005, all in large logo livery, together with a Class 03 and considerably fire damaged 31240, which was not withdrawn until 1990.

*Above left:* 56125, in blue with large logo, on coal hoppers passes Doncaster Black Carr sidings on 17th September 1985. In the background is newly ex-works Romanian-built 56017, now in grey with the large logo. 56017 emerged from the Electroputere factory and entered stock on 13th May 1977. It achieved large logo grey livery at its last major overhaul in 1985 and was withdrawn on 8th May 1992 after which it languished at Toton before being broken up there by Birds of Long Marston. 56125 was rather luckier. Built at Crewe Works and entering stock on 20th October 1983 in the livery seen here, after withdrawal it was stored at Immingham and sold to Fragonset Railways in July 2003. Moved to Derby in May 2004 it was reinstated in July to stored status, and overhauled at the RTC site in Derby. On 9th May it went to Barrow Hill for repainting into Fastline livery and it became 56303 on the 15th and hired to Jarvis Rail. It is now in all-over dark green and operated by the British-American Railway Services based at Washwood Heath, Birmingham.

*Below left:* Two months later, but at the same spot, 58018 hauls empty coal hoppers northwards. Built at Doncaster Works and entering stock in October 1984. On 21st May 1988 in was named High Marnham Power Station and retained this name until late 2001. In November 2003 it was allocated to the France Hire Pool and moved from store at Healey Mills to Eastleigh Works where it was put back into working order. It was outshopped in August 2005 and moved to the Channel Tunnel on the 23rd. It is painted in TSO (France) livery of yellow with a blue solebar and white roof. Allocated to Alizay, France, it is now stored with most others of its class.

*Above:* On 27th March 1988, with 47623 having failed at Sheffield, 47220, in Railfreight grey with large logo has taken over and hauls the diverted 13.17 York-Weston super Mare at Woodburn Junction, near where the present-day tram depot is located. The uniform rake of NSE-liveried Mark 1s is smart. 47220 was built as D1870 and entered stock on 11th June 1965. It was renumbered in February 1974 and in the mid-eighties acquired the large logo livery. It was named *RAPIER* unofficially at Tinsley on 21st October 1991 and was withdrawn in July 1993. Coopers Metals, Sheffield cut the loco up in April 1994.

*Above:* Railfreight grey liveried class 37/6s Nos 37686 and 37677 on an empty stone train from Balm Road Leeds to Tunstead on 16th May 1988 passing Meadowhall where the station now stands today. The cooling towers have gone and the shopping centre is now on the right hand side. No 37686 was new numbered D6872 on 6th September 1969 and became 37172 in 1974. It was rebuilt as a 37/5 in February 1987, becoming 37686. It was taken out of service in June 1999 and moved to France in July 1999 returning in June 2000. Sent to Springs Branch recovery centre and scrapped in April 2006. No 37677 was new on 19th April 1963 numbered D6821 and renumbered 37121 in February 1974 and after rebuilding 37677. Withdrawn 1st October 2007 and scrapped in October 2008.

*Below:* 37203, in large logo blue livery, and 37110 in Railfreight grey with Metals decals are pictured here on a steel train on 21st October 1989 on the Swinton avoiding line alongside the canal before Mexborough station. 37203 was new as D6903 on 19th April 1963 and became 37121 in May 1974 and was one of the few locos of the class allocated to the Southern Region, between 2005 and 2007. It spent time on Scottish passenger duties as well as Welsh and LMR. By the time of its withdrawal in November 2009, it was in Mainline Freight livery. It was moved by road to Ron Hull, Rotherham in December 2009 and broken up there on 4th May 2010. 37110 was new as D6810 to Darnall, Sheffield on 4th February 1963, becoming 37110 in February 1974. It spent time on passenger work in Scotland in 1984 and then East Anglian duties in the 1990s. It was withdrawn in July 1999 and was cut up by Raxstar at Immingham on 2nd May 2000.

56018 is seen on 29th April 1987 on a Merry-go-round working heading east past Shirebrook depot, where two Class 56s and a Class 58 can be seen awaiting their next duties. Another of the Romanian-built locos, 56018 entered service on 23rd August 1977. By 10 years later blue livery had changed to Railfreight grey with large logo as seen here. EWS red followed before withdrawal in February 2010. It was purchased by Europhoenix the following year and was re-registered for main line service in August 2013. Now operated by UK Rail Leasing, it is painted in Fertis livery of grey with red and blue solebar stripes. At the time of compiling it was stored at Leicester depot.

58032 is seen leaving West Burton Power station with an empty Merry-go-round train on 27th March 1990. Outshopped from Doncaster Works in September 1985 in the livery shown, it was named *Thoresby Colliery* on 31st October 1995, but the plates were removed by the end of 2001. Withdrawn on 12th January 2000, it was stored at Healey Mills. Reprieved for use in France it was restored to operating condition at Toton from July to October 2004 in Fertis livery and exported on 19th October 2004. It is presently stored at Alizay in ETF livery of yellow with white roof and green stripe on the solebar.

56024 is seen on railtour duty visiting Thoresby Colliery with the Hertfordshire Railtours' "Dukeries Collier" tour on 27th June 1992, which it shared with 20058+20168. 56024 was new from Electroputere, Romania on 15th June 1977 in Rail blue livery but had gained grey Large Logo colours by the time of this tour. It was withdrawn on 29th October 1996 and sent to Booth Roe, Rotherham for scrap the next month.

*Above:* 47227 is seen here on the Ely avoiding line with a summer Saturday holiday extra of blue and grey and NSE-liveried Mark 2s on 14th September 1991. New as D1903 on 9th September 1965 to Cardiff it worked mainly from Crewe and Tinsley. A few days after the photo, on 9th November, it was named *SALADIN*, which it retained until 6th May 1993 when withdrawn. It was sold to Coopers Metals, Sheffield and broken up in March 1994.

*Below:* 31196 and 31268 are seen at rest in Colchester depot on 16th June 1990. 31196 was new as D5620 on 2nd June 1960 and renumbered in 1973. It suffered major accident damage at Haughley Junction whilst hauling a TPO on 22nd June 1982 and it took 15 months for repairs to be completed. It had gained Dutch livery by the time of withdrawal on 26th February 1993 but it was not broken up until February 2001. 31268 was new as D5698 on 18th May 1961 and had a relatively uneventful life before withdrawal on 11th February 2000, being broken up by Thomson, Stockton the next month.

*Above:* Seen at the stabling point by the north end of Peterborough station is 47348 *St Christopher's Railway Home* on 27th July 1988. It was new as D1829 on 3rd March 1965 and was renumbered in November 1973. Shortly after the photo was taken it was repainted into revised Railfreight livery which it retained until stored after a derailment in March 2000. It was withdrawn in July 2002 and later moved to Brush, Loughborough to donate parts to 47756 after which it was stored for a while at Meldon Quarry. Ron Hull, Rotherham broke the loco up on 15th January 2007.

*Below:* 47186 *TINSLEY TMD SILVER JUBILEE 1965-1990* is seen taking a tank train east out of Ripple Lane yard, Dagenham on 29th March 1990, having received the name three weeks earlier. It was removed in July 2001 and the carried *Catcliffe Demon* from April 1993 to April 1999. It was new as D1781 on 17th November 1964 and became 47186 in February 1974. After the large logo livery, it gained Trainload Distribution and finally Railfreight Distribution before withdrawal in July 2002. Reinstated to Fragonset, Derby that November, it eventually went to EMR, Kingsbury in May 2007 where it was broken up on 5th December 2007.

# Southern Region

A wonderful view of pre-Eurostar Waterloo could be obtained from nearby flats as seen in this view of 47473 hauling a uniform rake of Mark 2s in NSE livery as the 17.06 to Exeter on 28th April 1989. It was new as D1601 on 6th July 1964 and spent a large portion of its career on the Western Region. It became 47473 in January 1974. It joined the Parcels sector in December 1990, InterCity in September 1992 and Railfreight Distribution in March 1994. It was stored from May 1995 and was disposed of by MRJ Phillips at Crewe Works in March 1998, although the vagaries of the system at the time meant it wasn't actually withdrawn until October that year.

*Above:* Here is 73105 on another Gatwick Express, passing Earlswood Station on 25th August 1984. It was new as E6011 on 5th December 1965, becoming 73105 in January 1974. It carried the name *Quadrant* between 4th November 1987 and August 1989. After large logo livery it carried InterCity colours from 1988 and then Dutch livery from 1992. It was stored in February 2000 and withdrawn in July 2001. Sold to Fragonset, it was moved to PeakRail in January 2003 for storage, it too went to the Battlefield Line. When Class 73s were being sourced for modernisation and upgrading, this one was sourced, and it was moved to Nemesis Rail in July 2013. It was still there in February 2014, looking rather derelict. However it has now been completely overhauled and modernised and renumbered 73969 for use with Caledonian Sleepers.

*Below:* On 10th March 1985, 50026 *Indomitable* passes Brookwood with the 11.10 Waterloo-Exeter with a rake of comfortable non-air conditioned Mark 2 coaches in blue and grey livery. It was new as D427 on 12th June 1968 and renumbered on 29th July 1973. It worked on the north end of the WCML before being displaced to the WR by electrification. It was named *Indomitable* in September 1978. It worked main line services on the Western and Southern routes to Exeter, passing to Network SouthEast whose livery it gained. Engine damage caused its withdrawal on 11th December 1990. It became part of the 'Operation Collingwood' project to preserve a number of these locos and was stored at Booth, Rotherham in 1992. A new owner acquired it and used parts from other scrap locos there to rebuild it. It was moved to the Mid Hants Railway in 1993 and then on to MoD Bicester. It was restored in 2007 and currently resides at Eastleigh. It is equipped for main line work and appears at Galas and on preserved lines.

Above: Class 50 No 50046 *Ajax* is seen working the 9.45 Exeter to Waterloo in Winchfield cutting, just before the station. It entered traffic on 2nd November 1968 numbered D446 and was named on 11th October 1978. It like all the class 50s initially worked expresses on the north section of the WCML, but on the completion of the electrification in 1974 the whole class were transferred to the Western region. It last worked on 5th November 1989 and donated its engine to No 50007 after withdrawal on 25th March 1992. It was sold to MC Metals at Glasgow and broken up.

*Below:* No 50046 *Ajax* is seen again this time just to the west of Wimbledon station with an up express from Exeter. Details of the locomotive are given in the previous caption.

*Above:* Class 73 No 73104 in large logo blue livery is departing Winchester with an up Bournemouth-Waterloo express and is seen from the road bridge just to the east of the station. Notice the new car park extension which today on weekdays is nearly always full. 73104 entered service in 1965 as E6010 in blue livery and received 73104 in March 1974. It was stored in April 1999, sold to Fragonset in October 2002 and then sent to Carnforth for long-term storage. It then moved to Barrow Hill and eventualy to the Mid-Hants Line in December 2003. Like No 73105 shown on page 52, it was bought and sent to Nemesis Rail and completely rebuilt into a Class 73/9 in 2015, numbered 73951, and painted in Network Rail yellow livery. 18th March 1988.

*Below:* 47603 *County of Somerset* is seen here passing through St Denys on the approaches to Southampton with a Freightliner train on 30th April 1988. New as D1967 on 16th October 1965 on the London Midland Region, it became 47267 in March 1974 and transferred to the Western. In December 1983 it was fitted with ETH and renumbered 47603, gaining large logo blue colours not long before this photo was taken. In December 1990 it was allocated to Parcels traffic and its nameplates removed in May 1992. It gained RES red livery, and was then renumbered 47745 in June 1994. Brian Blessed then named the loco *Royal London Society for the Blind* (with a smaller Braille version attached) on 24th September that year. Stored in May 2000, it was withdrawn in April 2004 and scrapped by Harry Needle at Toton in August 2004.

*Above:* 47290, in grey large logo livery, was pictured from the road bridge at the north end of Eastleigh station awaiting departure with an up Freightliner on 25th April 1986. New as D1990 to the North Eastern Region on 15th March 1966, it became 47290 in September 1973 in Rail blue livery. It soon gained the colours shown here, after which Trainload livery and eventually revised RFD colours were applied. Redundant in the early 2000s, it was in good enough condition for conversion to the Class 57 as 57316, gaining a reconditioned EMD engine, Class 56 traction motors and in December 2004 it was named *FAB 1 – Thunderbird*. West Coast Railways then took it on, and removed the name. It regained Rail blue for a while but in 2018 was working on the main line in WCR maroon.

*Below:* Electro-diesel 73139 heads the 10.00 Bournemouth-Waterloo through the junction at St Denys on 15th March 1988. New as E6046 on 23rd October 1966, it was renumbered 73139 in 1973. This livery replaced Rail blue, and in turn it gave way to InterCity main line colours. Pullman-style brown and cream adorned it in its later years and withdrawal came in April 2007. Having spent some time on the Weardale Railway in 2010, it is now owned by Railway Vehicle Engineering, and stored at Loram RTC, Derby.

*Above:* 73114 is seen with the VSOE Pullman rake just to the west of Southampton station whilst hauling a special to Beaulieu on 30th April 1988. It was outshopped as E6020 on 20th February 1966, becoming 73114 in 1973. It was allocated for use on the Gatwick Expresses and named *Stewarts Lane Traction Maintenance Depot* on 14th November 1994, losing it in July 1995. It gained InterCity by 1988 and was in Mainline blue by February 1995. In December 1998 it suffered derailment damage and was stored unserviceable. Withdrawal came on 3rd July 2001, but it was sold to Fragonset Railways and was moved to Peakrail for storage. It moved on to the Battlefield line in June 2004 where it regained large ogo blue livery and is now with Nemesis Rail.

*Below:* A view from over the tunnel just east of Southampton station on 1st May 1988 sees the 14.48 cross-country service to Newcastle leaving behind 47512. The rake of air-conditioned Mark 2 coaches is in a mix of blue & grey and InterCity colours. 47512 was new as D1958, entering traffic on 4th February 1967, one of the experimental batch (D1953-61) which were new in Rail Blue livery, so this loco only carried these two liveries. It became 47512 in 1973 and was allocated to Regional Railways services in December 1990 and Parcels a month later. Withdrawal came in October 1991 and sale to Booth-Roe, Rotherham in April 1993, where it was broken up in May 1994.

*Above:* Here is 73131, hauling an Up Channel Islands Boat Train through Bournemouth on 3rd August 1985. Ex-works Mark 1 coaches on the Southern Region always seemed to ride better on the Southern than elsewhere so a comfortable ride should follow. New on 10th July 1966 as E6038, it was named *County of Surrey* at Haslemere on 4th March 1988. It was intended to be renumbered 73255 in 1989 for Bournemouth line work but this never happened. The nameplates were removed in October 1993. It was taken out of use in August 2003 and withdrawn in January 2004. It was moved by road to Booth, Rotherham on 12th May 2004, and was scrapped by 25th August.

*Below:* 47801 pulls away from Andover station on 29th April 1992 heading the 8.40 Waterloo-Exeter. The formation for the former through lines can be clearly seen above the train. The loco was new as D1746 on 3rd July 1964 and was scheduled to be rebuilt with ETH during overhaul and was renumbered 47551 on 4th May 1974. A week later this was abandoned and 47153 substituted. ETH fitting happened on 22nd February 1965 and 47551 reapplied. Further upgrade to class 47/8 and renumbering to 47801 took place on 16th November 1993. it was stored in July 2002, withdrawn in April 2004 and broken up at Crewe diesel depot on 2nd March.

# Western Region

50047 *Swiftsure*, hauling the 13.33 Exeter-Waterloo on 10th August 1985, leaves Blackboy Tunnel as it approaches Exmouth Junction with a rake of blue & grey Mark 2A coaches. 50047 was new as D447 in December 1968 and was renumbered on 17th February 1974 and named on 26th May 1978. It last ran on 8th April 1988 on suffering engine problems and was withdrawn on the 13th. Vic Berry, Leicester broke it up between April and June 1989.

47441 is seen here passing Westbourne Park station on the approach to Paddington with an ECS of Mark 1 stock in NSE livery from Old Oak Common on 18th August 1991. It had been allocated to OOC the previous month for NSE Thames Line services. It lasted only until withdrawal on 15th December 1992 and languished until broken up by MRJ Phillips at Old Oak Common at the end of August 1997. In the background is the overhead M4 extension passing behind London Transport's Westbourne Park garage, whose yard at rail level is filled with minibuses used on routes 28 and 31 from early 1989.

56033 in large logo grey livery is approaching West Ealing off the Greenford branch with a stone train. It was noted in a complete condition when new on 1st May 1977 but was not taken into traffic at Toton until 2nd August 1977. In November 1977 it was damaged in an accident and was out of service for around four months. It was in BR blue livery when new and over the years carried the Construction and Transrail liveries. It was named *Shotton Paper Mill* at Chester Wagon repair depot on 18th December 1995, which it carried until April 2008. Withdrawal came in October 2003, after being placed in a strategic reserve pool at Thornaby depot from 7th April 2003.

*Above:* 47540 is seen here on 16th November 1989 with an up empty Permanent Way train at Slough, taken from the bridge west of the station. New as D1723 on 17th March 1964 it was allocated 47132 but did not carry it, becoming 47540 on 17th October 1974. At the time of the picture it was allocated to Old Oak Common but on 24th August 1990 it was allocated to Civil Engineers work and renumbered 47975 and named *The Institution of Civil Engineers* on 2nd September 1991 retaining it until it reverted to 47540 on 18th December 1995. It was allocated to Strategic Reserve in June 1998 and withdrawn in November 2002. It was preserved at Sinderby, North Yorkshire from September 2003 and to Heanor Haulage yard at Langley Mill in May 2009, thence to the Weardale Railway that September. It was eventually towed to T J Thomson, Stockton in March 2016 and scrapped.

*Below:* Here 56039 with an up stone train passes the yards at the west end of Slough on 28th April 1990. It was new on 7th February 1978 and was in two-tone Railfreight grey, and then grey large logo livery by 1988, and the red band by the time of this picture. From 19th July 1994 until 31st July 1997 it carried the name *ABP Port of Hull*. It was in Loadhaul livery when named. Withdrawn on 29th September 2003 it was taken to T J Thomson, Stockton by road on 29th January 2004 and broken up that April.

*Above:* With Didcot Power Station in the background, 47457 *Gazelle* heads the 08.20 Paddington-Oxford NSE train with a mixed rake of Mark 1 and 2 stock when approaching Culham station on 19th October 1991. It was new as D1577 on 25th April 1964 and became 47457 in March 1974, being named *Ben Line* from 13th February 1986 until April 1990, after which it gained the unofficial name *Gazelle* from July 1990 to 21st February 1992. It was scrapped later that year.

*Below:* 47801 is seen again at Pangbourne on a Cross Country service from the south coast to Manchester on 25th April 1990. Its history is on page 58.

With the Malvern Hills forming the background, and the site of Worcester steam shed behind the train, 47816 is at Worcester Tunnel Junction with the diverted 08.20 Poole-Birmingham on 5th August 1990. The Hereford line is to the right. Most of the train is InterCity liveried air-conditioned Mark 2s with one earlier Mark 2 in blue and grey. D1650 was new on 9th January 1965 and became 47066 in January 1974. It was upgraded to Class 47/4 as 47661 in October 1986 and then to 47816 on 23rd February 1989. It later gained the name *Bristol Bath Road Quality Approved* on 26th May 1995, losing it in January 2003. After Large logo livery, it carried InterCity Swallow colours and then First Great Western green with gold stripe, later losing the stripe. It ceased to be hired to Virgin Trains in December 2004, and went to Freightliner, being stopped due to the lack of OTMR equipment on 24th January 2008. Since then it has languished in Basford Hall yard, Crewe, gradually deteriorating in appearance, still being there in 2018.

Here is 37116, with its unofficial name *COMET*, which it carried from November 1989, being seen on an up Permanent Way train at Droitwich on 5th August 1990. New on 1st March 1963 as D6816 and renumbered to 37116 in 1973, it gained its unofficial name on 20th November 1989 and *Sister Dora* was attached on 25th February 1996, losing it in January 2001. It was withdrawn in February 2007 and passed for preservation to the Chinnor & Princes Risborough Railway, where it was used until sale to Colas in January 2014, being reinstated to main line use. It was moved to Washwood Heath on 28th and then on to Barrow Hill for overhaul on 2nd July 2015 returning to use on 16th October 2015 in Colas colours.

*Above:* 47444 *University of Nottingham* is seen here leaving Hereford with the 16.35 Cardiff-Chester on 31st May 1987. It was new as D1560 on 11th March 1964 and became 47444 in August 1973. It carried its name between 14th May 1981 and November 1990 when it was withdrawn. It was eventually cut up by MRJ Phillips at Crewe Works in July 1995.

*Below:* Pioneer Class 50 50050 *Fearless* is seen here leaving Bristol Temple Meads with the 07.00 Oxford-Paignton of Mark 1 coaches on 6th July 1985 with King class 4-6-0 6023 *King Edward II* in the dock in the background to the left of Brunel's famous trainshed. D400 was new on 17th October 1967 for use on the north part of the West Coast Main Line. When that was electrified all the class was transferred to the Western Region to replace diesel hydraulics. All were refurbished between 1979 and 1984 and after the first six, all were repainted in the large logo livery, to which the others later were repainted. Withdrawal of the class started in 1987 and by the start of the 1990s use on the Great Western route was gradually declining with replacement by Cl.47/7 and then DMUs. D400 was named *Fearless* on 27th August 1978 and carried it until April 1991. The loco was then repainted into a close approximation of its livery when new which included losing its name. It was withdrawn on 26th March 1994 after another repaint back to large logo livery. Preservation followed by the D400 Fund, and it then passed to Boden Rail and is Main Line Certified as we went to press.

In its heyday Severn Tunnel Junction was a mecca for diesel enthusiasts. Class 50 No 50039 *Implacable* is shown heading the 12.06 Cardiff-Portsmouth service on 1st August 1987. It is formed of four Mark 1 coaches and a Mark 2 BFK in the middle. In the background is a row of at least nine class 37s, several class 47s and a number of class 08 shunters. Also in view are some carriages and engineers vehicles.

With Llanwern Steel Works in the background, Newport East Usk Junction is the setting on 2nd March 1987 for a steel train hauled by 37901 *Mirrlees Pioneer*. A Class 38 was proposed in the 1980s using a Mirrlees MB275T engine coupled to a Brush alternator, and four Class 37s were fitted with this equipment as mobile testbeds with new bogies and extra ballast weights. 37150 became 37901 on 30th October 1986 and the original four were joined by two more, with different power/alternator combination, before the Class 38 was abandoned. The class was regularly used for Llanwern steel trains until displaced by more powerful Class 66s. D6850 was new on 1st July 1963 and became 37150 in April 1974. After displacement, it was withdrawn in June 2002 and saved for preservation, working on the Llangollen line from 2003, then visiting various other preserved lines before being acquired by Colas Rail in May 2016, presently stored awaiting possible restoration to use. It retains the livery shown with the addition of a red skirt.

*Above:* Here is another view of 37901 *Mirrlees Pioneer*, this time with an up ballast train on the west side of Newport, leaving Hillfield Tunnel on 4th August 1987.

*Below:* 4th August 1987. A little further west still, at Gaer Junction and about to enter Hillfield Tunnel, is 37255, leaving the Valleys lines with a Merry-go-round train on the same day. New as D6955 on 6th January 1965 it was renumbered in April 1974. It spent some time after its last works overhaul on Cambrian Coast trains but received this livery at a major exam in 1987. It later went to Immingham, and then Thornaby before passenger use in Scotland in 1994. TransRail duty from Bescot followed and it gained Civil Engineers livery. It was withdrawn in January 1999. A brief reinstatement followed later that year and it was sold to Fragonset Railways in October 2002 and then purchased for use on the Great Central Railway. External condition deteriorated and it was stored, but was moved to Nemesis Rail by road on 6th January 2016.

Moving to Bristol, here we see 47638 *County of Kent* on 11th July 1987 heading the Saturdays only 11.33 Penzance-Newcastle cross country service on Ashley Down bank at Narroways Hill Junction, where the Severn Beach branch leaves the main line. D1653 was new on 16th January 1965, becoming 47069 in January 1974. Selected for rebuilding as a Class 47/4, it became 47638 on 12th February 1986, gaining large logo livery. It was named on 20th June 1986 and chosen for further upgrading with long range tanks to Class 47/8 as 47845 on 24th November 1989. After large logo livery it gained Intercity Swallow livery and Virgin Trains red. It was then chosen for re-engining with a refurbished EMD engine and reconditioned alternator for use on Thunderbird duties for Virgin West Coast. It was reclassified as Class 57, and allocated 57611 in May 2002, revised to 57301 later that month when painted in Virgin Thunderbird livery. The name *Scott Tracy – Thunderbird* was applied on 17th June 2002, being removed in September 2011. On being made redundant from these duties, it passed to Direct Rail Services (DRS) and renamed *Goliath* on 6th October 2014. It remains in traffic in DRS blue livery.

*Above:* Seen from the bridge over the lines at the east end of Taunton station is class 50 No 50049 *Defiance* working the 9.24 Paignton to Birmingham New Street. It was the last of the class to be built and numbered D449 in December 1968. It was named on 2nd May 1978 and was the only member of the class to receive Railfreight Distribution livery. It was withdrawn on 16th August 1991, bought by the Class 50 society and returned to main line working.

*Below:* The second Class 50 built, as D401 on 9th December 1967, 50001 received this number in 1973 and was named *Dreadnought* on 10th April 1978. It was the fourth of the class to be refurbished, outshopped on 9th April 1980, retaining Rail Blue livery, and then gained large logo livery in August 1984 and later NSE darker blue livery. It was withdrawn on 19th April 1991, and became part of the abortive Operation Collingwood project to preserve a number of the locos. In the event, when it closed in 2002, 50001 was sent for scrap to Booth-Roe, Rotherham for spare parts that December. It is seen here leaving Whiteball Tunnel's west end with the 10.18 Paddington-Paignton on 7th September 1985.

50044 *Exeter* is seen here near Torquay on the Kingswear branch with the 08.50 Cardiff-Paignton on 7th July 1985. It was new as D444 on 11th October 1968 and renumbered in 1973. Named *Exeter* on 26th April 1978 and refurbished on 29th April 1982, it ran its last train in December 1990 after suffering a main generator failure. The 28th of its class withdrawn, on 11th January 1991, it was saved for preservation on the Severn Valley Railway, during which time it was Main line registered, and received a non-authentic BR two-tone green livery with D444 number. Whilst on railtour duty in 2012 it suffered an engine failure and is now being restored with a similar engine acquired from a Portuguese Class 1800 loco.

Class 50 No 50010 *Monarch* is seen at Dainton summit at the west end of the tunnel on 7th July 1985 heading the 9.40 Plymouth-Paignton which reversed at Newton Abbot on Sundays. It entered service on 21st February numbered D410 and was named on 16th March 1978. After a serious failure it was withdrawn on 27th September 1988 and scrapped at Laira depot in February 1992.

*Above:* 50036 *Victorious* is seen on 25th August 1987 on the 15.57 Plymouth-Penzance at the east end of Lostwithiel station. D436 entered traffic on 12th August 1968 and was renumbered in 1973. Naming took place on 16th May 1978 and refurbishment into large logo livery on 18th June 1981. It was withdrawn on 12th April 1991, still in large logo livery, and was broken up at Booth Roe, Rotherham on 3rd July 1992.

*Below:* 50018 *Vanguard* is crossing Moorswater viaduct in Cornwall heading an empty stock working 6th September 1985. The locomotive entered service as D418 in April 1968. It was named on 6th April 1978, gaining NSE livery later. It was withdrawn on 22nd July 1991. It was broken up by M C Metals Ltd at Glasgow in January 1993.

*Above:* 37675 heads an up China Clay train at Restormel, Cornwall on 28th August 1987. New as D6864 on 22nd August 1963, it was one of the locos which gained a full yellow end on green livery in August 1969 and was renumbered 37164 in February 1974 and then rebuilt to Class 37/6 specification in large logo grey livery, and renumbered 37675 on 29th May 1987, being named *William Cookworthy* in August 1987, losing it in January 1994. It was allocated to Railfreight Distribution in 1990, Regional Railways North West in 1994 and Transrail in 1996 and then to EWS at Old Oak Common in January 2002. It was stored in September 2007 and withdrawn on 8th August 2010 and cut up at EMR, Kingsbury two months later.

*Below:* Here we see Par station from the road bridge at its east end on 29th August 1987 with 50030 hauling the Saturdays only 17.17 Newquay-Plymouth with its rake of mostly air-conditioned coaches, two of which have gained the new InterCity livery. In the background above the middle of the train can be seen one of the cream and brown liveried "Skippers", introduced in 1985/86 to replace 'heritage' DMUs. They are now known as Class 142 "Pacers" but were removed from this area after operating difficulties. 50030 *Repulse* was new as D430 on 25th June 1968 and was renumbered in 1973. Named on 10th April 1978, it became the 48th of the class to receive refurbishment, outshopped on 14th September 1983. It ran its last train in April 1992 and it was withdrawn on the 8th due to main generator failure. It became part of Operation Collingwood and was moved to the Pontypool & Blaenavon Railway for store with 50029 *Renown*. On the collapse of the project, both were purchased by the Renown-Repulse Group and moved to Peak Rail with a cosmetic repaint. It is under restoration.

# London Midland Region

Having been subjected to the special Stratford treatment, immaculate 47583 leaves Chesterfield southbound on 8th May 1982 with a Manchester-Harwich boat train, seen where the former Great Central line crossed this Midland route. The loco was new as D1767 on 29th October 1964 and became 47172 in March 1974. Selected for upgrading to Class 47/4 it became 47583 on 9th November 1980 and in honour of the Royal Wedding in 1981 received a special version of large logo livery where the horizontals extended to the far cab door and the main logo was in red, white and blue. It was named *County of Hertfordshire* in December 1981 and retained it until December 1993. On conversion to Class 47/7 as 47734 on 27th March 1996 it became *Crewe Diesel Depot Quality Approved*, keeping this until December 2004. After large logo livery it received both versions of NSE livery and then RES red, retained when it became 47734. It was withdrawn in February 2007 and broken up at EMR, Kingsbury in May 2008.

On 9th August 1988 two class 56s are passing Tupton junction south of Chesterfield heading for Toton depot. On the right is a steel train from the north east heading for South Wales headed by class 37/5s Nos 37503 and 37504 of Thornaby depot. 56007 and 56021 were built by Electroputere Craiova in Romania in April and June 1977. 56007 was withdrawn in September 2010 and passed to Riveria Trains in 2011 and is now owned by UK Rail Leasing and stored, still in original blue livery at Leicester. 56021 was withdrawn in June 2008 and passed to the Harry Needle Railway Co who resold it to T J Thomson at Stockton where it was broken up in July 2009. The class 37s were new as D6717 and D6739 in February 1974. Both worked in Anglia and then Scotland. They received heavy general overhauls and emerged as class 37/5s, outshopped on 5th and 14th March 1986. 37504 was then selected as one of the locomotives for use on the Channel Tunnel and was renumbered 37603 on 2nd May 1996. 37503 passed to Harry Needle in March 2011 and then to DRS in January 2014 and to Europhoenix Uk in March 2016. It was then stored in EWS livery at Leicester and at Loram Derby.

*Above:* On 4th July 1989, 20137 in grey large logo livery and blue 20178 head north at Hasland, south of Chesterfield on the slow line, with the site of the old steam shed in the background. At this time, 20137 was named *Murray B. Hofmeyr* which it carried between 4th June 1987 and July 1991. It was built as D8137 on 12th April 1966 and renumbered in 1973. It was withdrawn on 1st December 1992 and purchased privately for use on the Gloucestershire-Warwickshire Railway where it was restored to working order in 1995. It is still running there in green livery as D8137. 20178 was not so fortunate. Built as D8178 on 16th December 1966 and renumbered in 1973 it was withdrawn five months after this picture was taken and it was broken up by MC Metals in Glasgow in June 1992.

*Below:* 56128 was new on 18th December 1983 and withdrawn in August 2005. It is owned by British American Railway Services and is at their Washwood Heath premises. It was allocated number 56313 but the work has not been proceeded with. It was named *West Burton Power Station* between February 1993 and 12th March 1995. It is seen hauling an up coal train on 28th August 1984, along the Midland Main Line in the Erewash Valley at Langley Mill in the Nottinghamshire Coalfield.

*Above:* On 12th October 1984, we see a line-up of almost-new Class 58s, 58010, 58014, 58007, 58003 and 58013. 58003/7 were built in July and November 1983, 58010/3/4 in February, March and April 1984. 58003 was named *Markham Colliery* on 5th November 1988, 58007 *Drakelow Power Station* on 25th August 1990 and 58014 *Didcot Power Station* on 11th June 1988, this being removed in 2001. 58003/14 were withdrawn on 29th November 1999 and 17th November 2000 and both were scrapped at EMR, Kingsbury in August 2010. The others were withdrawn between 1999 and 2001 as well, and exported for use in France, where they are now stored.

*Below:* On 24th March 47340 hauls 86219 and its train, the diverted 10.40 Euston-Shrewsbury at Washwood Heath, Birmingham, with the elevated M6 in the background. 47340 was new as D1821 on 10th March 1965 and renumbered 47340 in March 1974. Always a Midlands loco, it was withdrawn in June 1998, but it had already been broken up by MRJ Phillips at Crewe Works that March.

*Above:* A Freightliner from Southampton to Birmingham Lawley Street is passing Camp Hill, nearing its destination. Freight trains in the opposite direction often needed bankers in the past. Here 58040 is in charge on 2nd August 1986, having only entered service on 18th March that year. On 20th September it was named *Cottam Power Station*. It only had a short life on BR, being withdrawn on 7th December 1999. After being restored, it was allocated to work in France, being exported on 13th November 2004. It is currently stored at Alizay, Rouen.

*Below:* Here 56063 heads a down stone train at Glendon Junction, north of Kettering on 28th June 1986. It is stationary, having just failed and is awaiting assistance. 56063 was new on 6th September 1979 and named *Bardon Hill* from 6th October 1996 to July 1999. It was withdrawn on 31st August 2005 and scrapped by Booth, Rotherham in November 2007.

Pioneer class 47 No 47401 is seen approaching Grindleford station from the west heading the 11.41 Manchester Piccadilly to Hull on 2nd April 1986. The entrance to Totley tunnel is at the platform end; it is 6231 yards long (5697m). The history of 47401 is on page 38. Also present in the siding is class 31/1 No 31302 in large logo grey livery working a Permanent Way train. It entered service numbered D5832 on 26th April 1962 and was renumbered on 2nd February 1974. Withdrawal came on 14th January 2000 although it had been broken up in 1999 at Wigan Recovery depot.

A light load for a Class 47! On 6th May 1988, 47358 heads down the gradient at Buxworth Curve between Chinley and New Mills. A favourite location for photographers that formerly had four tracks. 47358 was new as D1877, to traffic on 11th June 1965 and was renumbered in February 1974. It received the unofficial name *Ivanhoe* on 5th May 1994, by which time it had received Freightliner Railfreight Trainload grey with a red triangle. It was withdrawn on 28th February 2007 and moved to T J Thomson, Stockton in August that year. It was broken up there in March 2009.

Two photos of 50012 *Benbow* hauling Hertfordshire Rail Tours' "The Derbyshire Dingle" tour on a snowy 8th February 1986. In the first picture, the tour is passing Peak Forest en route to Buxton and in the second it has just left Buxton. The tour had started from Paddington behind 50016 *Barham* as far as Derby where 50012 took over for the rest of the tour, except where 45022 hauled it from Buxton Single Access into the station. 50012 then returned the tour to Paddington. 50012 was new as D412 on 27th March 1968 and renumbered in 1973. The name *Benbow* was applied on 3rd April 1978. Withdrawal came on 16th January 1989 following a main generator failure, and it was broken up on 1st July 1989 at Vic Berry, Leicester.

*Above:* On 19th June 1992, 47356 heads the 16.23 Bolton to St Pancras mail vans, some of which are now in the new RES livery. It is passing Agecroft power station, which closed in March 1993, and shows the cooling towers which were demolished on 8th May 1994. The unit being passed is a Class 150/1 No 150134 in the dedicated Greater Manchester Transport colours. 47356 was new as D1875 on 2nd July 1965 and was renumbered in March 1974. From 3rd June 1995 it carried the unofficial name *THE GURKHA* which it carried until rebuilt as the prototype Class 57 57001, returning to traffic on 17th July 1998, when it gained the new Freightliner green livery and the name *Freightliner Pioneer*, which it lost on 31st December 2007. It was then taken on by the West Coast Railway Co in January 2011 and returned to service in WCRC maroon.

*Below:* On 29th May 1993, 47458 hauls a diverted InterCity express from the north to Liverpool past St Helens and the Pilkington Glass Works with its old aerial rope way. 47458 is attached to DVT 82118, with its electric locomotive on the rear end. 47458's history is on page 30.

On 18th June 1988, the 13.23 Cardiff to Liverpool Lime Street emerges into the station from the deep cutting leading down from Edge Hill headed by 37431 *Sir Powys/County of Powys* and formed of early Mark 2 coaches. 37431 was new as D6972 on 26th March 1965 and became 37272 (first use of the number) in March 1974. It was rebuilt as a Class 37/4, 37431 on Heavy General repair, emerging on 18th April 1986 in large logo livery. It was named on 17th June 1987. It was allocated to Provincial's Cardiff pool in January 1989 and gained InterCity Main Line livery in October 1990. Its name was removed in April 1991 and *Bullidae* applied on 31st May 1991, retaining this until April 1993. Transfer to Scotland followed in July 1991. It passed to Transrail in March 1995 and was stored unserviceable in March 1996, returning to traffic by April 1998. It was withdrawn in April 1999 and arrived at Wigan CRDC for component recovery on 11th November 1999 and cut up on 5th January 2000 with the last bits removed on 14th August.

Rare motive power and train at Oldham Mumps on the occasion of Oldham Athletic's appearance at Wembley for the Football League Cup Final against Nottingham Forest on 29th April 1990. (They lost 1-0!). 47099 was built as D1686 and entered service on 8th November 1963 and was renumbered on 4th February 1974. It is here seen in its final livery of Railfreight grey with large logo. Withdrawn on 12th November 1991 it was broken up at Booth, Rotherham in April 1994. Not only has the loco gone, both the Mark 2 BSOs and 2 of the Mark 1 Opens have gone (three remain on main line service and three are preserved) but so has the station and indeed the line as well. Manchester Metrolink extended its network over the line to Oldham, but diverted away from the heavy rail route in favour of a line through the town centre, rejoining the old line several hundred yards behind the camera. The Oldham loop line closed on 3rd October 2009 for rebuilding and reopened from Manchester Victoria as far as Oldham Mumps, temporarily using the old rail alignment at Oldham, with a halt at the former station site. The line was extended in stages to Rochdale Town Centre by 31st March 2014, with the loop through Oldham town centre opening on 27th January 2014.

47449 is hauling a Crewe Basford Hall to Leeds, Stourton Freightliner between Saddleworth and Diggle, heading towards the Standedge tunnels on 5th May 1990. There were four tracks here formerly, the two on the left that have been lifted formed the Micklehurst loop to Stalybridge. D1566 was new to traffic on 23rd March 1964 and was renumbered 47449 in March 1974 and was outshopped from Crewe Works in large logo blue in March 1986. It was named *Oribi* on 13th July 1990, and was de-named on 14th May 1993. It was withdrawn that month and entered preservation, owned by Peter Waterman as a Rail Charter Services locomotive. In 1996 the Llangollen Diesel Group purchased it for use on the Llangollen Railway, in original two-tone green with full yellow ends as D1566 from 2002, when it was named *Orion*. After five years out of use it was restored to traffic in 2017 in rail blue with yellow ends and small logo as 1566.

On 2nd July 1988, the 09.40 Euston-Aberystwyth has reversed in platform 4 at Shrewsbury and 37429 *Eisteddfod Genedlaethol* and 37430 *Cwmbran* have been attached for the journey over the Cambrian route. The train, formed of a set of NSE-liveried Mark 1 coaches, is seen leaving Shrewsbury from Severn Bridge Signal Box, which still supervises the scene in 2018. It is heading for the North & West route towards Hereford and Newport, but will turn right onto Cambrian lines about a mile further on at Sutton Bridge Junction, which is also where the Severn Valley branch once left to go to Bridgnorth. 37429 was new as D6600, to traffic on 26th August 1965. 37300 was applied on 15th November 1973 and it was rebuilt to Class 37/4 as 37429 on 3rd March 1986. It was named *Sir Dyfed/County of Dyfed* (one side only for each) from 2nd April 1987 to 1st August, and it was replaced by *Eisteddfod Genedlaethol* on 4th, carrying it until April 1993 and again from July 1993 to December 2001. It received a light overhaul and repaint into Regional Railways livery in January 1991, and a further intermediate overhaul at Doncaster Works in May 1996. It was stored in September 2002 and withdrawn on 5th February 2008, having been sold to EMR, Kingsbury the previous month. It was broken up there on 8th February 2008. 37430 was new as D6965 on 3rd February 1965 and became 37265 in March 1974. It was rebuilt to Class 37/4 as 37430 with large logo livery on 25th March 1986 and received the name *Cwmbran* on 11th May 1986. After a light overhaul at Glasgow Works from April 1990 it received InterCity Mainline livery. Further overhauls were at Doncaster in April 1995. It worked its last train on 27th March 2000 and was stored next day. In April 2003 it was allocated for component recovery, sold in January 2008 (officially withdrawn that March) and moved to EMR, Kingsbury on 8th March, being cut up on 14th May.

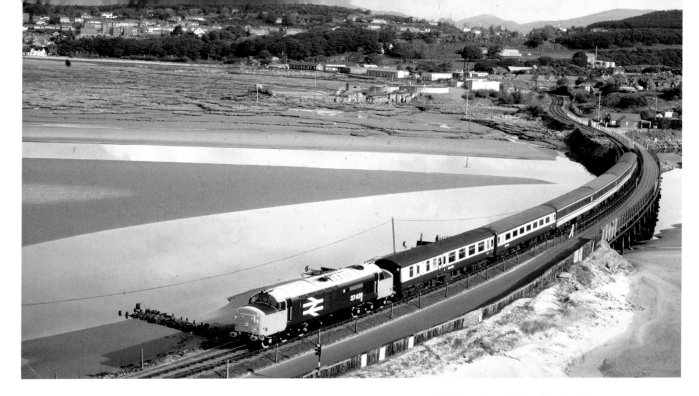

*Above:* On 16th May 1987, the 08.00 Pwllheli-Euston is seen crossing the Pont Brewit trestle bridge shared with a local road at Penrhyndeudraeth headed by ex-works 37428, which had been named *David Lloyd George* that day. The bridge has been replaced by a new structure for rail, opened in 2014 and road in 2015. New as D6981 on 12th May 1965, it was renumbered to 37281 in May 1974 and rebuilt to Class 37/4 as 37428 on 16th February 1986. A new coat of paint followed for the naming, and light overhauls followed in May 1991 and March 1996. It was repainted in Royal Scotsman claret livery in April 1998, losing its name. *THE ROYAL SCOTSMAN* name was applied on 14th May, losing it in April 2001. Between May 2002 and December 2004 it carried the name *Loch Long* on one side and *Loch Awe* on the other. It went to Tactical reserve in December 2003 and store in February 2004. Passed to disposal in October 2009 it was moved to Booth, Rotherham on 18th December 2009. It was taken to Long Marston in April 2010 and back to Booths on 7th November 2012. Finally withdrawn in February 2013 and cut up on 4th March.

*Below:* Here we see 37429 again, this time after leaving Fairbourne on the climb to Friog and its rock shelters with the 08.00 Pwllheli-Euston on 21st May 1988, formed of a rake of InterCity liveried air conditioned Mark 2s. Its history was given on page 88.

*Above:* On 22nd July 1995, the rake of Regional Railways liveried stock forming the 17.24 Crewe-Bangor, headed by 37408 *Loch Rannoch*, is seen crossing the River Dee outside Chester on the remaining used viaduct, the ex-GWR one, the one to the left, ex-LMS, disused after reduction from four tracks to two. The racecourse is in the background and the view is taken from the road bridge leading to the golf course. 37408's details are on page 31.

*Below:* The 09.50 Euston-Holyhead "Irish Mail" hauled by 47519 is seen approaching Mostyn on 30th September 1989. In the background is *TSS Duke of Lancaster*, moored at Llanerch-y-Mor. It was built by Harland & Wolff, Belfast in 1955 and it was designed for the Heysham-Belfast route for the BTC and then Sealink, and for cruises around Europe. In 1970 it ceased cruise work and was rebuilt to carry cars via stern doors. When that service ceased on 5th April 1975 it was used briefly between Fishguard and Rosslare and then settled down on the Holyhead to Dun Laoghaire route until 1978 when it was laid up at Barrow. In 1979 it was purchased by Empirewise for use as a "Fun Ship". Constant battles with the authorities saw the ship closed in 2004 since when the ship has rested there, gradually deteriorating externally, but still in good internal condition. In 2012 it was used as an art gallery for graffiti artists, but in 2017 both sides were painted black! 47519 was new as D1102, one of the last Brush Type 4s built, on 9th September 1966. It became 47519 in February 1974 and received large logo livery in the mid-1980s. In 1995, it was allocated names *Restormel* and *Resolven Grange*, but neither was carried. From 1992 it was allocated for Parcels work and under RES control, it was repainted in an approximation of the original BR two-tone green with yellow ends. Withdrawn in June 2005, having been stripped at CRDC, Wigan, it was sold to T J Thomson, Stockton and scrapped on 8th October.

*Above:* 47452 in ex-works condition is seen leaving Llandudno Junction on the 13.15 Holyhead-Euston on 11th October 1986, a time when InterCity 'Raspberry Ripple' livery was coming into use. New as D1569 on 31st March 1964, it became 47452 in May 1974. On 24th June 1984 it derailed and overturned when heading the 19.50 Aberdeen-Kings Cross sleeper, taking a 50mph curve at about 90mph. It was taken to Crewe Works and took 2 years and 3 months to rebuild, and was outshopped a few days before this photo was taken. Between May 1988 and June 1991 it was named *Aycliffe* and it was withdrawn on 16th August 1991. It was eventually cut up by MRJ Phillips at Old Oak Common in April 1997.

*Below:* Here the 17.05 Holyhead-Coventry leaves Holyhead station on 29th April 1989 and climbs the short 1 in 75 gradient past the stabling point, formerly the steam shed, where 47345, 47637 and 08739 are stabled. Beginning service as D1584 on 16th May 1964, it was allocated 47021, but this was not carried and it was outshopped from conversion to Class 47/4 as 47531 on 21st May 1974. It was allocated to Civil Engineers' use as 47974 from 11th June 1990 and carried firstly their colours, then the 'Dutch' livery. Between May 1991 and June 1992 it was named *The Permanent Way Institution*. Ceasing this use it reverted to 47531 on 24th June 1992. It then passed to RES in its livery and carried the name *Respite* from September 1993 until June 2003, being renumbered 47775 in December 1993. It was stored unserviceable from July 2001 and withdrawn in April 2004. The Harry Needle Railway Company broke it up at Crewe DMD on 21st April 2006.

The 09.20 Euston-Holyhead is seen leaving the tubular bridge over the Conway estuary with the castle in the background on 20th September 1986. New as D1677 on 24th April 1965, it was named *THOR* on 29th August 1966 with plates transferred from scrapped D1671. It was renumbered 47091 in March 1974 and rebuilt to Cl.47/4 in February 1986 as 47637, when it received large logo livery, and to 47846 in November 1989. The name was removed between September 1975 and April 1985 and was retained on 47647 and 47846 but it was removed at the end of 2012. It gained InterCity Swallow livery on conversion to 47846, and subsequently both versions of Great Western and then First Great Western livery. Off lease in June 2002, it was converted to Class 57 with the refurbished EMD engine and also gained Dellner couplers as 57308 *Tin Tin – Thunderbirds* and Virgin Trains Thunderbird livery. On ceasing this work in 2012 it passed to DRS in its Compass livery for continued DRS/Virgin Thunderbird use. In August 2013 it was renamed *County of Staffordshire*, losing this in March 2017, and it is now named *Jamie Ferguson*.

*Above:* 47378 is seen departing from Scotchman's Bridge, Greenholme, while descending Shap bank on 17th October 1986. It was built as D1897 and entered traffic on 2nd September 1965. It was renumbered 47378 in March 1974 and then to 47386 on 5th July 1994, reverting to 47378 on 7th August 1995. After large logo grey livery it carried Trainload Distribution livery and was carrying that when withdrawn in August 1998 and cut up at Booth-Roe, Rotherham the next month.

*Below:* 47446 leads the "Garstang Tripper" special from Preston to Edinburgh on 13th May 1989 through Beckfoot, close to where the Low Gill line used to leave the main line. 47446 was new as D1563 on 4th April 1964 and became 47446 on 9th April 1974. After an accident, a cab salvaged from D1562 after its damage was fitted to this loco. It was named *GALTEE MORE* from 11th December 1990 until withdrawal. In June 1991 it was allocated to NSE work and then withdrawn on 24th February 1992 and disposed of to MRJ Phillips at Old Oak Common in May 1997.

47407 heads a Thames-Eden Charter run by InterCity as it passes Barron Wood in the Eden Valley on 13th May 1989. One of the first batch of the class, it entered service on 18th June 1963 and was renumbered 47407 in March 1974 and then named *Aycliffe* between 9th November 1984 and May 1988. It was withdrawn in August 1990 and eventually broken up by MRJ Phillips at Frodingham in December 1995.

47503 heads the diverted 10.55 Stranraer-Euston across the embankment before Ribblehead station on the Settle & Carlisle line, with the viaduct behind the train. It started life as D1946 on 6th July 1966 and became 47503 in May 1974. It was named The Geordie from May 1988 to June 1991 and then *Heaton Traincare Depot* from 18th May 1993. It was allocated to Parcels sector, and then Rail Express Systems (RES) in whose livery it was painted, and renumbered 47771 in June 1994. It became EWS property and last ran in February 2000. It was sold to the Class 47 Preservation Society in August 2002 and moved to the Colne Valley Railway for restoration on 25th June 2003, the nameplates being removed by then. During rebuilding, metal thieves struck and set back the repair and it is still to return to service.